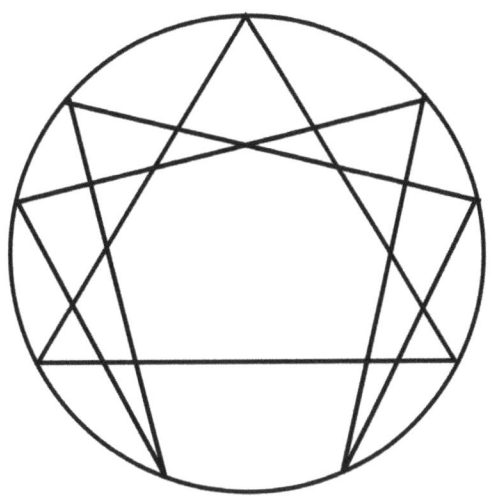

YOUR ENNEAGRAM AND MONEY
WORKBOOK

KHARA CROSWAITE BRINDLE
HANNAH DEGROOT

Guide Point North Publishing
Colorado, U.S.A.

Guide Point North Publishing
An imprint of Journey Institute Press,
a division of 50 in 52 Journey, Inc.
www.journeyinstitutepress.org

Library of Congress Control Number: Availalble upon request
Names: Brindle, Khara Croswaite
Degroot, Hannah
Title: Your Enneagram and Money, Workbook
Description: Colorado: Guide Point North Publishing, 2025

Identifiers: ISBN 978-1-964754-28-4 (paperback)
978-1-964754-29-1(ebook/kindle)

Subjects: BISAC: BUSINESS & ECONOMICS / Personal Finance / Money Management |
SELF-HELP / Personal Growth / Success |
BODY, MIND & SPIRIT / Numerology

First Edition

Printed in the United States of America

1 2 9 21 22 37 50 65 77 90

This book is typeset in EB Garamond / Oswald

Cover Design by WiggleB Studios

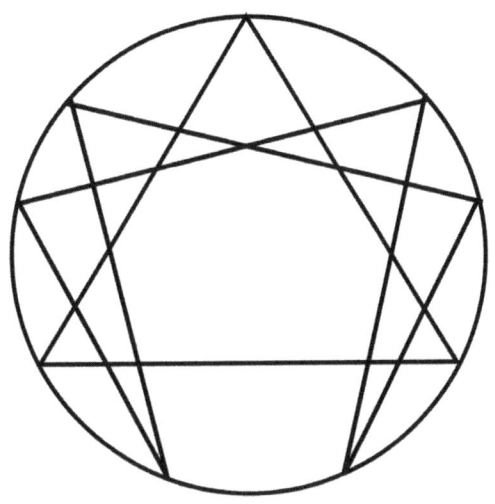

Part I

Know Your Money Story

Uncover Your Money Beliefs

A person has, on average, 50-200 money beliefs, according to Rick Kahler, Financial Therapist and a founding member of the Financial Therapy Association. Money beliefs impact our emotions, thoughts, and behaviors with money. What are some of your money beliefs? For example, what comes up for you when you think about:

• Holiday spending/gifts
• Car buying
• Homeownership
• Student loans
• Taxes
• Expensive airfare
• Attending a Destination Wedding
• Job loss
• Inheritance
• Welfare
• Medical emergency
• Family loss and grief
• Retirement

_____

_____

_____

_____

_____

_____

Now that you've recorded some beliefs. Map them on a spectrum of negative to positive. Which beliefs feel more negative to you? Why? Which beliefs feel more positive? What neutral money beliefs would land in the middle of your line?

Negative   Positive

Negative   Positive

Enneagram Edge: How might some of these beliefs be connected to your dominant type/subtype?

Financial Therapy Focus: Notice any body sensations as you write down or say money beliefs out loud. This technique can help you map them visually as positive or negative in your life.

Finding Your Negative Money Script

Inspired by Dr. Brad Klontz, founder of Klontz Money Script ® Inventory, let's take a quick quiz to find your script and what it could mean.

What's My (Negative) Money Script?

1. You get a bonus at work. You decide to:
    a. Buy that new pair of shoes you've been eyeing.
    b. Put it straight into your 401K.
    c. Text your besties, "we're going out and I'm buying!"
    d. What bonus? You haven't checked your bank account balance in weeks.

2. You're calculating your quarterly taxes for your business this year and find yourself:
    a. Excited to upgrade to the latest phone you've been wanting.
    b. Feeling confident that you've put enough aside for when taxes are due.
    c. Hoping for a tax return to fund your next much-needed vacation.
    d. Starting to sweat. Can't you put this off until next month?

3. Your parents want to sit down and talk about their estate planning as part of their retirement. You respond by:
    a. Giving advice on what they should do with all their money.
    b. Worrying about how to maintain the estate if they ask you to.
    c. Asking how you can help celebrate their hard work.
    d. Brushing them off, saying you are busy for several weeks.

4. You stumble across a video on the importance of running financial reports as a business owner. Your reaction is:
   a. Anticipation about your next big purchase.
   b. Eagerness to invest your profits for your future.
   c. Determination to work even harder to see those numbers grow.
   d. An upset stomach and your mind going blank.

5. You are following a colleague online that you admire, and recently see them sharing about a new investment that's making them more money. You:
   a. Invest in the same program, barely looking at the price tag.
   b. Roll your eyes. How can they justify the cost when they should save that money?
   c. Do a bit of research then call us your finance friend for advice.
   d. Unfollow them. Seeing their money content is stressing you out.

Mostly a's: Money Status "I've worked hard for my money, I want to show it."
Mostly b's: Money Vigilant "Don't spend money, save it!"
Mostly c's: Money Focus "More money would make me happier."
Mostly d's: Money Avoidant "I don't want to think or talk about money."

Money Status
"I've worked hard for my money, I want to show it."

- Desire to display wealth publicly
- More often seen in young adults
- Can be a tool to see something beyond physical disability
- Most likely Enneagram Sevens and Eights

Money Vigilant
"Don't spend money, save it!"

- Doesn't spend money lavishly or gamble
- High anxiety about money, must save it never spend it
- Difficulty enjoying money due to feelings of guilt after purchases
- Most likely Enneagram Ones and Fives

Money Focus
"More money would make me happier."

- May experience hoarding
- May spend in large amounts to show love to others
- Increased risk of workaholism
- Most likely Enneagram Threes, Fours, Sixes, Sevens, and Eights

Money Avoidant
"I don't want to think or talk about money."

* Doesn't ask for raises or promotions
* Minimizes own abilities and paid opportunities
* Goes hand-in-hand with Noble Poverty
* Most likely Enneagram Twos, Fours, and Nines

Enneagram Edge: How might these beliefs be connected to your core fear?

Financial Therapy Focus: How can your negative money script inform your warning signs for noble poverty and scarcity in the next exercise?

Recognizing Noble Poverty and Signs of Scarcity

Noble poverty is the experience of sacrificing our own financial well-being for the benefit of others. **Scarcity** is a belief that there isn't enough, which results in other self-sacrificing behaviors. You could say noble poverty and scarcity are close cousins. So what are the warning signs that either of them are driving your money decisions? Map out your warning signs according to your five domains of self as well as financial behaviors for added clarity on your current relationship with money.

Examples
Physical (i.e. muscle tension, migraines, stomach distress, sleep disruption)

Emotional (i.e. irritability, hyperfocus, anger, sadness)

Relational (i.e. micromanaging, picking fights, judgmental, lack of self-trust, financial gatekeeping, resentment, people-pleasing)

Mental (rumination, fixation, hypervigilance, compulsive checking, optimizing, spiraling)

Spiritual (self-doubt, insecurity, comparison, envy, fatigue)

Financial (budgeting, vigilance, hoarding, avoidance)

Physical	Emotional

Relational	Mental

Spiritual	Financial

Enneagram Edge: How might domains be impacted by your dominant type/subtype?

Financial Therapy Focus: Getting stuck on what you look like in noble poverty or scarcity? Consider the vulnerability and bravery that come from asking people closest to you how you show up in order to fill in the gaps.

Finding Your Healthy Money Script

What's My Healthy Money Script?

Answer the questions below to explore the healthier script you want to embody as your heal your relationship with money!

1. You're getting ready to head to work when your car breaks down. The mechanic quotes you $1200 in repairs. You think:
   a. I'll remain hopeful that I can make the extra cash this month.
   b. I'll take on a new client to make the extra funds and keep my budget where it is.
   c. This is why I have a periodic expenses account. I'll move the money over now to pay for the repairs.
   d. I can't afford that. I'll have to put it on the credit card which makes me feel awful.

2. You're walking across the parking lot of the grocery store when you find a crumpled $20 bill on the ground. Your response:
   a. This is the $20 I needed to give myself permission to get _____ on my grocery list this week. Thanks universe!
   b. This feels perfectly timed after spending $20 on a gift for the party this weekend.
   c. Neat! I'm feeling good with my money so I'm going to brighten someone's day here at the store.
   d. Oh no! It's awful that someone lost it and it's not nearly enough money to make a difference with my current financial stress.

3. It's July, which is a slower month of earning for you in your small business. Your family wants to take advantage of the time off with the kids being home from school, and they are asking for a family vacation to have a week together. Your response is to:
   a. Have each family member craft a wish list of things they'd want to do for a week and pick the week to confirm staff coverage in your absence.
   b. Prioritize a week of low-key activities and connection with the family and start speaking to staff about coordinating their time off too.
   c. Confirm business funds are present for Paid Time Off and offer a paid week off to staff the same week for team rest and restoration.
   d. Find yourself stressed. How are you supposed to afford a vacation when revenue is dwindling?

4. You're finishing up a delicious dinner out with your best friend when they discover they've misplaced their card to pay their portion. You respond by:
   a. Reassuring them that you've got this one and that their card will be found in no time.
   b. Offering to pay for this meal knowing they can reciprocate by buying next time.
   c. Paying for the meal and leaving a nice tip for the server who added to the enjoyable experience for both you and your best friend.
   d. Starting to panic for your friend and for yourself now that the only option is for you to pay for the whole meal.

5. Your partner comes home talking about burnout and wants to take a spontaneous weekend trip away. Your reaction is to:
   a. Get excited, start packing your bags, knowing you'll figure out where to stay once you get there.
   b. Recognize you just finished a top earning week at work and think it could pay for this trip.
   c. Identify the trip location, purchase your activities and lodging, and move the funds over from your vacation account.
   d. Get angry. Why would they think this trip could happen right now when money feels tight?

Mostly As: Money Optimism "What it comes to money, it will all work out."
Mostly Bs: Money Harmony "Money comes and money goes, money flows."
Mostly Cs: Money Plentiful "There is enough money."
Mostly Ds: Money Scarcity "There is not enough money." (the opposite of healthy money scripts)

Money Optimism
"When it comes to money, It will all work out."

- Resourceful
- Take on bigger risks with no mental angst
- Gut feeling, intuition reduces money anxiety
- Most likely Enneagram Fours and Sevens

Money Harmony
"Money comes and money goes, money flows."

- Embraces the flow and movement of money
- Does not seek stagnation in their spending and saving
- Holds confidence that money will come in when needed
- Most likely Enneagram Ones, Twos, Sixes, and Nines

Money Plentiful
"There is enough money."

- Uses money as a tool
- Ever-evolving with their money
- Takes risks
- Most likely Enneagram Threes, Fives, Eights

Enneagram Edge: The 9 Enneagram Virtues are the antidote to the Types' Passions. How might your Virtue help you better conceptualize your Healthy Money Script?

 *Financial Therapy Focus: Are you attracted to one script over the others? Even if you didn't test as a certain type in the quiz, what's one script you'd like to embody more often and why?*

Attachment Styles and Money

There are three attachment styles in relationships, Secure, Anxious, and Avoidant. Since we've established that you can have a relationship with money, which attachment style might you have with your finances?

Secure Attachment is the ideal attachment type, embodying reassurance, safety, and connection.

Anxious Attachment describes a dynamic of insecurity and self-doubt, along with questioning of the validity of the relationship, our self-worth, and worthiness to the point of acting out from intense anxiety.

Avoidant Attachment describes a disconnected style where a person may operate as if they don't want or need anyone or anything, responding to vulnerability and intimacy with avoidance.

My attachment style with money is: _____

Attachment Reflection Questions:
1. *Which attachment style do you have with money? How do you know?*
2. *Which attachment style do you have with a partner or spouse? How do you know?*
3. *What attachment style would you like to have with money? Why?*
4. *If money could talk, what would you want it to say to you when you need reassurance?*
5. *What can a partner or spouse say (or do) for you that is comforting and helps you emotionally regulate?*
6. *What can you do for yourself when your attachment style is driving your behaviors?*
7. *How might you view your attachment style through the lens of your Enneagram type? What does that bring to light for you? What do you want to consciously work on?*

_____

_____

_____

_____

_____

_____

_____

_____

_____

Questions for Connection:
1. *What triggers a conflict or fight with your partner/spouse about money?*
2. *What feelings come up for you in the conflict?*
3. *What does your inner critic say about you/your abilities in the conflict?*
4. *Where do you feel that criticism in your body?*
5. *What does the fight say about your relationship?*
6. *What reassurance are you needing from your partner in the conflict to help you regulate?*
7. *How can you voice that need for reassurance to help you feel heard?*
8. *How might your dominant Enneagram type or your partner's dominant Enneagram type be playing into these conflicts and emotions?*
9. *What could you do to show your partner compassion after viewing the conflict through the lens of their Enneagram type?*

_____

_____

_____

_____

_____

_____

_____

_____

_____

_____

_____

_____

Financial Therapy Focus: Your partner can support co-regulation when you are triggered by money. Share a few things with your partner that can help you. Do you need a hug? Proximity and deep breaths? Eye contact and reassuring words? A shoulder to cry on? Letting them know what works best for you can give them a roadmap for other times you might need support.

Money as a Partner

Take a look at the above image. On the right side of the infinity symbol is you; your thoughts, your feelings, your behaviors. On the left side is money, how it thinks, feels, and behaves as if it were a partner in your story. Imagine a line separating your half of the infinity symbol and money's side. This line represents an incident that sets this conflict between you and money in motion. We've just described the Couples Conflict Cycle of *Emotionally Focused Couples Therapy (EFCT)*. The incident could be something like an unpaid bill, a medical crisis, exceeding a budget, or paying a credit card. Money can be the hero, the villain, or the enabler in your relationship.

1. When you think about the incident, what thoughts come up for you? Map them on the infinity symbol.
2. When you think about the thoughts, what feelings come with them? Map them on the infinity symbol.
3. When you think about the feelings, what behaviors are the result? Map them on the infinity symbol.
4. How does money respond to your behaviors? Does it help or hurt?
5. If money is adding to the conflict, what response from money would make things better?
6. How can your thoughts, feelings, and behaviors change the conflict pattern for the better?

_____

_____

_____

_____

_____

_____

_____

_____

_____

_____

_____

_____

_____

_____

_____

_____

_____

_____

_____

_____

_____

_____

_____

Enneagram Edge: If money was typed with the Enneagram, what Type would be most challenging for you to relate to and why?

What type would be easiest for you to connect with and why (i.e. If my money was typed as an Enneagram 7, I'd connect with it easily because it would embrace spontaneity with spending. If my money was typed as a 6, I would find it challenging because of the anxiety they bring to the table)?

What might this reveal to you about specific growth areas in your own life?

Financial Therapy Focus: Where in this image do you have control to make changes? Where can the negative pattern or conflict pattern be disrupted in support of a healthier partnership with money?

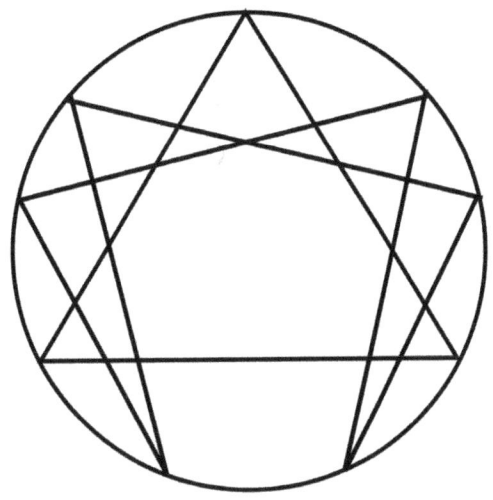

Part II
Healing Financial Trauma

Emotional Freedom Technique (EFT)

Emotional Freedom Technique (EFT) is a tapping tool aimed to regulate the nervous system through stimulation of various pressure points. What makes it approachable for financial trauma is that it's a tool for the present, and there is no need to reframe our negative thoughts or emotions while engaging in the practice of EFT.

Step 1: Review the list of EFT tapping points
1. The heel of your hand
2. Your inner eyebrow
3. Your temple
4. The place where your under eye meets your cheekbone
5. The skin between your nose and your lip
6. The skin between your chin and your lip
7. Your collarbone
8. Your lowest rib at your side
9. The top of your head

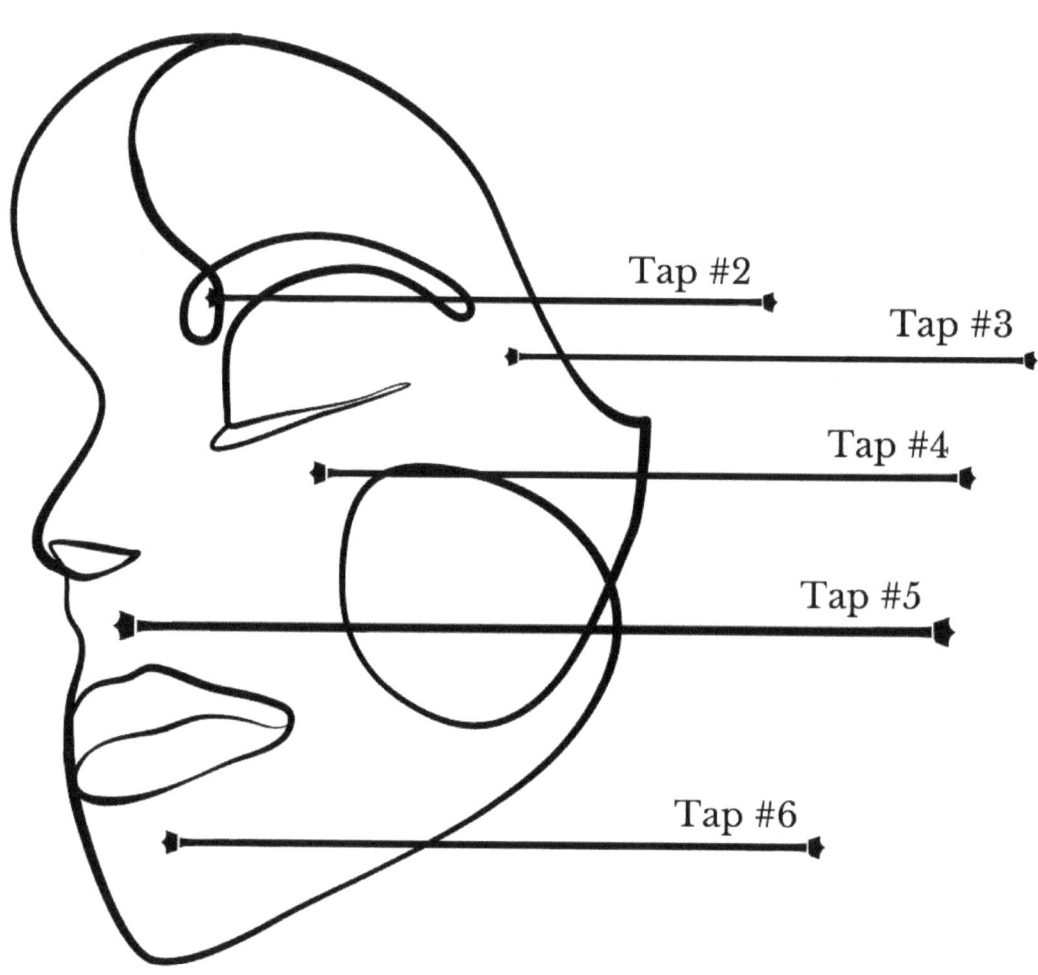

Step 2: Identify any negative or charged sensations in your body as you recall your worries or stressors with money. Begin by tapping the heel of your hand with your opposite hand. Name out loud your worries or stressors connected to money, without censoring, reframing, or revising your word choice.

Step 3: Move down the list of tapping points as you express your emotions out loud. Allow your worries or thoughts to come to you as you tap.

Step 4: Complete three or more cycles of tapping as you move down the tapping points on your body. Notice any shifts in the negative sensations that were present at the beginning of the exercise. Notice which tapping spots you found most comforting or liked best. Repeat your tapping cycle as needed for the desired positive shift in sensations and emotions.

Enneagram Edge: Enneagram Body Types (8, 9 and 1): The best way to process emotions is through body-work like this exercise which may increase the intensity for you. Notice any shifts in your emotions. Remember to ground yourself after doing any kind of body work - get outside and go for a walk or face the sun for a few minutes.

Enneagram Heart Types (2, 3 and 4): Your emotions can be overwhelming/scary at times. Doing body exercises like these can help you process those emotions in deeper ways. Remember that your heart center and body center are connected and that focusing on one area will impact the other. Take a break from journaling or verbal processing to try this exercise.

Enneagram Head Types (5, 6 and 7): This exercise may feel completely foreign to you. Don't overthink it. Try and get into the sensation of your body with your emotions and picture all of the energy from your head moving down through your body. What is it like to give your mind a break? Consider engaging in body work like this when you find yourself over-analyzing.

Financial Therapy Focus: EFT is a great tool for addressing emotions, stressors, and trauma triggers that are happening in the present. What did you discover?

Core Beliefs Exercise

A core beliefs exercise serves to look at the past as well as the present, and isn't something to dive into without proper time and space. Why? It feels more charged and vulnerable to sit in beliefs that we tend to suppress deep down inside, often hidden and rooted at the core of who we are.

Step 1: Grab a piece of paper or a journal. Self-worth is deep rooted in beliefs we carry based on the earliest experiences we have in life. To make these core beliefs more approachable to self-discovery, let's use a tree visual.

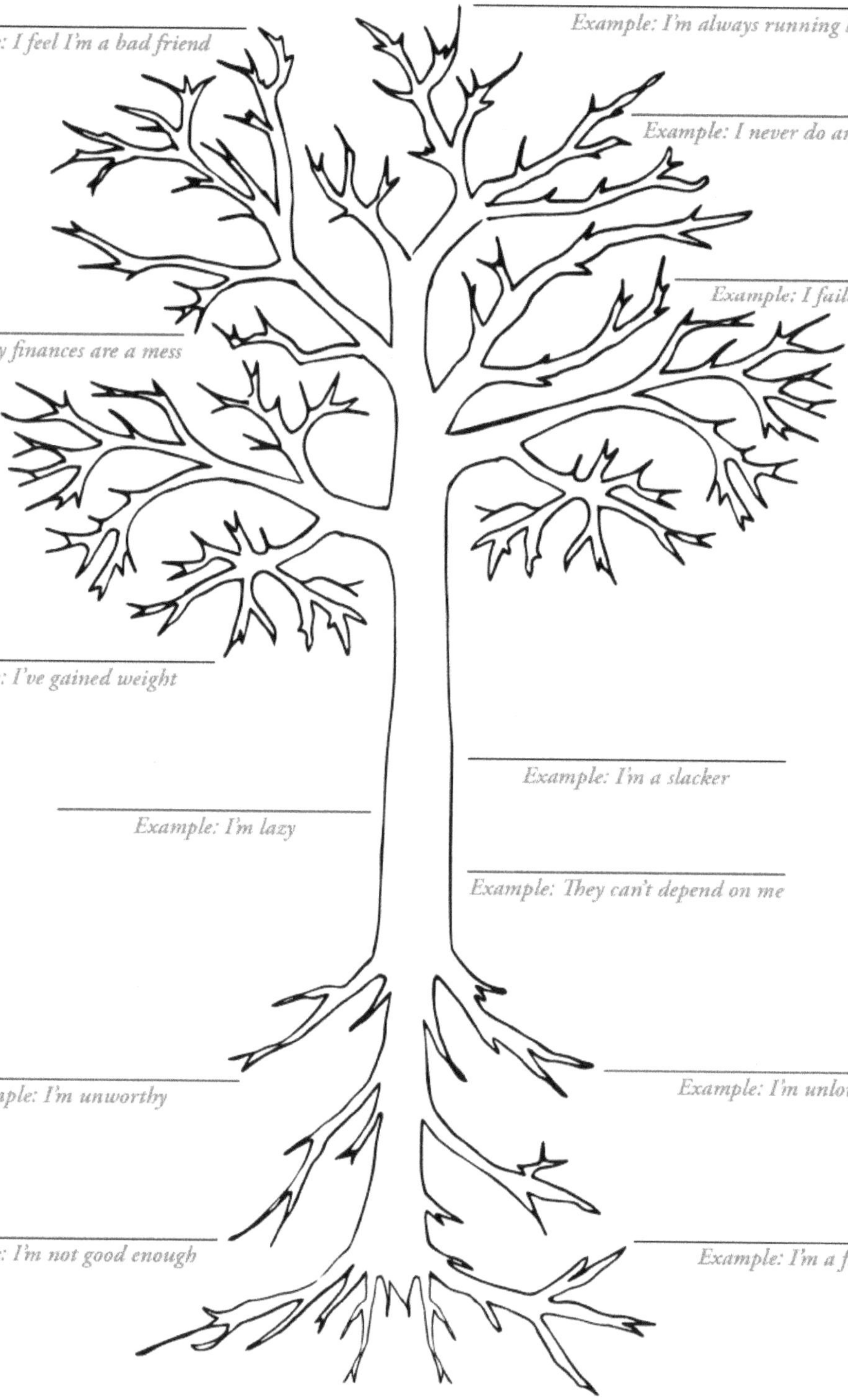

Example: I feel I'm a bad friend

Example: I'm always running late

Example: I never do anything right

Example: My finances are a mess

Example: I failed the test

Example: I've gained weight

Example: I'm a slacker

Example: I'm lazy

Example: They can't depend on me

Example: I'm unworthy

Example: I'm unlovable

Example: I'm not good enough

Example: I'm a failure

Step 2: The worries and anxieties we are consciously aware of are the leaves of the tree. These are the things we can easily verbalize such as stressors and concerns. Things like "I'm always broke. I feel like a bad partner when I can't stick to our budget. I'm always running behind on bills. I don't speak up for what I want financially." What are your worries and anxieties related to money? Write them in the leaves of the tree.

Step 3: Going deeper cognitively, we ask ourselves what these thoughts say about us, which gets us to the trunk of our tree. We may recognize thoughts like, "I'm stupid with money. I can't be trusted with money. I need someone else to manage my money." Write down key phrases or thoughts on the trunk of your tree.

Step 4: We continue to ask ourselves the question, "if this is true about me, what does this say about me?" to go even deeper, in order to get to the roots of the tree. The roots represent the negative core beliefs that drive our behaviors and can feel painful to explore. Negative core beliefs sound like "I am unlovable. I'm a failure. I'm unworthy." Capture your negative core beliefs in the roots of your tree.

Step 5: Now that you are aware of your negative core beliefs, what would you prefer to believe? Write the opposite of your negative core beliefs or another, more positive belief to the side of your tree. Make sure it's an 'I' statement! Try on statements like "I am loveable as I am. I'm trying the best I can. I am worthy." Which new beliefs are easier to embrace or accept?

Enneagram Edge: How might each of these influence your beliefs about money?
The Enneagram Fixations are a form of limiting beliefs for each type. Consider how these unique mental preoccupations might be playing into your money beliefs:

Type 1. Resentment - nothing is good enough and I cannot accept what is
Type 2. Flattery - I need to make others like me
Type 3. Vanity - I need succeed and be admired for my accomplishments
Type 4. Melancholy - I am missing something
Type 5. Stinginess - I don't have enough / I don't need a lot
Type 6. Cowardice - I am not ready or able
Type 7. Planning - I need to control how my life looks so I am always happy
Type 8. Vengeance - Life is not fair and I can make it better
Type 9. Indolence - I don't matter; I need to be less/do less

Financial Therapy Focus: What core beliefs are you trying to amplify? Keep them visual on your bathroom mirror or a post-it note at your work space for a gentle reminder.

Dear Money Letter

Inspired by Jen Sincero's book You are a Badass at Making Money, we love the emotional punch a hand-written letter to money can bring to financial trauma healing.

Option 1: Write a letter to money breaking up with it and removing its power from your life

By writing a letter to money as if it were an abusive relationship you want to end, the writer can feel empowered to cultivate a new relationship with money, one rooted in self-trust, empowerment, and healthier dynamics with finances. Here's one example:

Dear Money,
I've come to the realization that this isn't working anymore. The power you've held over me is hurting my mental health and I need a change. I'm tired of feeling shame every time I see my credit card statements. The embarrassment I feel when I can't pay the bills on time is excruciating. I don't like feeling stupid and I will no longer allow you to treat me as if I'm less than. I'm ready to have a better relationship with money, and you are not it. It's over.

Sincerely, _____

_____

_____

_____

_____

_____

_____

Option 2: Write an authentic, emotional letter to money, then have money write a letter of response to you

What do you want to say to money? What themes would money embody in their response to you? What compassion or protection could they convey in a healed, healthy relationship with you?

Dear Money,
I've come to the realization that this isn't working anymore. The power you've held over me is ....

Sincerely, _____

Dear_____,

I hear what you are saying and I realize I've gone about this all wrong. I've made you feel shame and embarrassment, hoping it would prevent you from spending. I've attempted to protect you from debt, but recognize now how that has backfired. I promised security and haven't delivered on that promise. My contributions in your life have made you question yourself and your abilities, and I'm sorry. You've shared how you struggle to trust me and I know I can do this differently. I hope you'll give me a chance to show you that our relationship can be better, one built on trust and open communication. I really want to try.

Yours, Money

_____

_____

_____

_____

_____

_____

Enneagram Edge: *What would this letter look like if you included your Enneagram type's Passion? What would you want to say to your passion and how do you think it would respond?*

Financial Therapy Focus: *What would you want money to say in a healthy relationship with you? From a place of secure attachment? As a supportive partner?*

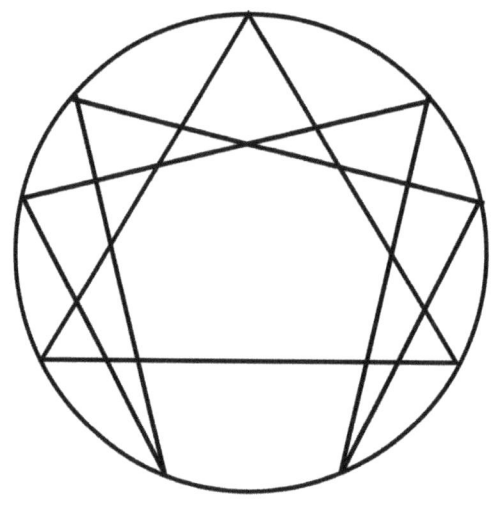

Part III

Momentum with Money

Money Word Association

Notice what thoughts, sensations, and beliefs that come to mind and write them down for each of the words below:

1. Loan
2. Savings
3. Retirement
4. Poor
5. Rich

Thoughts	Sensations	Beliefs

Map out where your current beliefs about each land on a spectrum.

Negative   Positive

What do you prefer to believe about each of these words? Write them down and map them on the image above to see the emotional shift you are growing towards.

Loans _____

Savings _____

Retirement _____

Poor _____

Rich _____

Enneagram Edge:

Enneagram Body Types: Notice where you are storing any emotions related to this exercise. What do you need to do to process these as they are not just body sensations but deeper emotions? Trust your intuition.

Enneagram Heart Types: Your emotions are being stored in your body. Where do you notice them showing up? How can you lean into that sensation in order to process it more fully?

Enneagram Head Types: Try not to rely on logic and thinking when engaging in this exercise. Do a grounding exercise to become present in your body and try to connect with your feelings. When you notice your head taking over, continue grounding to empty your mind.

Financial Therapy Focus: Consider revisiting your word association over time to see how beliefs and sensations are evolving. Are they landing more neutral over time?

Money Barometer

Imagine you have an amount of money in an account that has no purpose. It's just there. Record your thoughts, feelings, and sensations for each one below.

You have $1,000 in an account with no purpose, it's just there.

_____

_____

$5,000 in an account with no purpose, it's just there.

_____

_____

$10,000 in an account with no purpose, it's just there.

_____

_____

$25,000 in an account with no purpose, it's just there.

_____

_____

$50,000 in an account with no purpose, it's just there.

_____

_____

$100,000 in an account with no purpose, it's just there.

_____

_____

$500,000 in an account with no purpose, it's just there.

_____

_____

What are you noticing in your responses to each amount? Is there an amount where things shifted for you? What amount opens up all possibilities?

Enneagram Edge:
Did you do this exercise consciously or unconsciously? When you become conscious of your Type's Passion and your Instinct's influence, how might you view this exercise differently? What do you want to be conscious of as you go back through and complete it again with intentionality through this lens?

Financial Therapy Focus: The amount is less important than the beliefs attached to it. What amount allows you to live freely in your money story? Why?

Make a Money Meeting

Talking about money regularly by yourself or with others can remove some of the charge of money shame and guilt. However, structure matters to make the meeting worthwhile instead of painful and shameful.

Explore the Following:

The most relaxing setting to have a money meeting is (my house, outside, the office, kitchen table, window seat, etc.)

_____

The best time of day to have a money meeting is (morning, afternoon, late at night, etc.)

_____

The length of time of a money meeting I can commit to, to start is (5 minutes, 20 minutes, an hour, etc.)

_____

The materials that I need to feel prepared for a money meeting are (my bank login, a notebook, snacks, stress ball, etc.)

_____

The clothing that makes me feel comfortable and confident for a money meeting is (sweats, favorite shirt, slippers, etc.)

_____

The date I will have my first money meeting is

_____

My celebration for completing my money meeting will be

_____

Enneagram Edge:
Self-Preservation Enneagram Subtype: Risk being vulnerable with someone about your finances. What does it feel like to ask for help?

Social Enneagram Subtype: Resist the urge to consult with multiple people before your meeting. Come in with your own ideas before engaging a partner, family member, friend, or professional.

One-to-One Enneagram Subtype: What boundaries might be helpful for this meeting? How can you regulate your emotions before, during, and after the meeting?

 *Financial Therapy Focus: For many people, money meetings have been historically stressful. How can a small money meeting move your emotional meter from stressed out to neutral? How can your five senses make a money meeting more pleasant?*

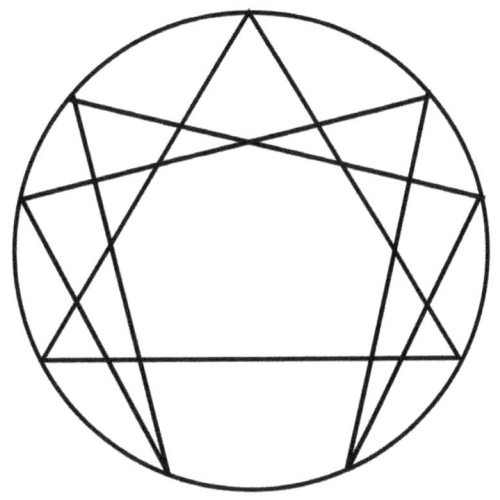

Part IV

Strategies for Saving

Renaming for Reframing

When you think about the word wealth what comes to mind?
1. What do you see when you think about wealth?
2. What emotions are connected to the word wealth?
3. What messages have you received from others about wealth?
4. What beliefs do you have about wealth?

When you think about the words credit cards what comes to mind?
1. What do you see when you think about credit cards?
2. What emotions are connected to the words credit cards?
3. What messages have you received from others about credit cards?
4. What beliefs do you have about credit cards?

When you think about the word savings what comes to mind?
1. What do you see when you think about savings?
2. What emotions are connected to the word savings?
3. What messages have you received from others about savings?
4. What beliefs do you have about savings?

For many, these words can feel charged and bring up self-criticism and shame. Consider the emotional impact of renaming your accounts.

How different would it feel to see 'Freedom,' 'Cushion,' or 'Family Trip to Florida' instead of 'Savings'?

What about 'Life-Changing Trip to Tuscany' for travel fees on your credit card or 'Starting a Family' for charges related to IVF or 'Peace of Mind' after a medical emergency?

Now it's your turn! What is a word or phrase that lightens the load of not seeing your savings and/or credit card balances where you want them?

1. Write down possible word/phrase options.

2. Check in with your body when you say them out loud. Warm and fuzzy? Calm? Anxious? Keep brainstorming until you find options that are positive or neutral.

3. Try them on for size by renaming your accounts in your online banking system. What do you notice when you see the new names as you login?

4. Adjust and revise as you go!

Possible words or phrases	Body/Emotions/Sensations

Enneagram Edge:

Self-Preservation Enneagram Subtype: When you think about saving, you may feel a sense of relief. How can you reframe saving to be something you are working towards instead of preparing for or fighting against?

Social Enneagram Subtype: Saving for yourself also allows you to engage with others. How can you connect your individual goals to the greater community you're a part of to find more motivation to save?

One-to-One Enneagram Subtype: How can you make saving a competition with yourself? Try and gamify the process to see what you can accomplish.

Financial Therapy Focus: Consider two or more accounts for savings if possible. This supports money motivation in having a savings experience that feels closer and more possible (in one account) over something 20 years away (in another account).

Paid Time Off (PTO) Account

When you work for yourself, you may struggle to take time off because you don't get PTO from an employer. This exercise is a game-changer for self-employed individuals and people who need an extra cushion of funds for sick time or leave when PTO isn't available.

Self-funded PTO accounts are magical for:
• Planned time away
• Maternity/paternity leave
• Unexpected illness
• Mental health days
• Family/kids illness or needs
• Slumps or slowdowns in workflow

Close your eyes and imagine that a family member comes down with a highly contagious virus, causing you to miss out on work for a week to stay home with them. You only have three days of PTO available to use, which is adding to your stress on top of not wanting to get sick yourself. Write down some of your thoughts and feelings in response to this scenario.

_____

_____

_____

_____

_____

Now close your eyes and imagine that you have funds set aside for sick days and family needs. As you are sitting at home making sure your loved one is getting enough fluids and rest to recover, you take five minutes to move over funds from your PTO account into your checking account, just in time to beef up your light paycheck from missing out on work. Write down some of your thoughts and feelings now.

_____

_____

_____

_____

_____

Is a PTO account something you want to implement? Would you call it PTO or something else? We've heard names like rainy day fund, emergency fund, and cushion as some examples. What amount would you move into the account on a monthly basis to ensure it remains funded for times in need?

Enneagram Edge:
Self-Preservation Enneagram Subtype: Try and find balance. You may be tempted to overindulge on self-care days or you may be motivated to keep working so you don't miss out on an opportunity to make more money. Whichever side you fall on, what does it look like to intentionally lean the other way?

Social Enneagram Subtype: How could creating this fund allow you to better connect with others? Be intentional about using it for yourself even as you are motivated to be with or use it for other people.

One-to-One Enneagram Subtype: How would this fund serve your ability to maintain the energy and intensity with which you love to live your life? What boundaries might you need to put in place surrounding this fund?

Financial Therapy Focus: Which would feel better to you, moving an amount into this account monthly yourself or an autopay amount sent monthly? Why?

Fill Your Buckets Funds

There are money management models out there that ensure small business owners (including helpers!) are getting paid for the things you do. Our strategy is called the Fill Your Buckets Funds.

Monthly Income - Monthly Expenses (including paying yourself!) = Fill Your Buckets Funds (FYBF).

Example: $6,000 monthly income - $4,500 expenses = $1,500 FYBF.

What would you do with extra money? Notice what you've written down and how they may connect to your values (i.e. things you find important to spend money on).

_____

_____

_____

_____

Small-spend joys are items or experiences we spend money on that don't break the bank. What are some of your small-spend joys that bring happiness and fight off deprivation with saving money?

_____

_____

_____

_____

Enneagram Edge:
Self-Preservation Enneagram Subtype: How can you allocate money to various accounts that are not restricted to savings or emergency funds? What other priorities do you have and what would it be like to have money go to these areas of your life?

Social Enneagram Subtype: Have an account that's for yourself as well as one for your business/family. You often think in terms of the group, so how can you balance prioritizing yourself as well as your community or organization?

One-to-One Enneagram Subtype: Consider the long-term goals you have for yourself. How can you put more money away to enjoy at a later time instead of right now?

Financial Therapy Focus: *What would balance look like between saving and small-spend joys? How do you give yourself permission to spend on small items from a place of pleasure, happiness, or joy?*

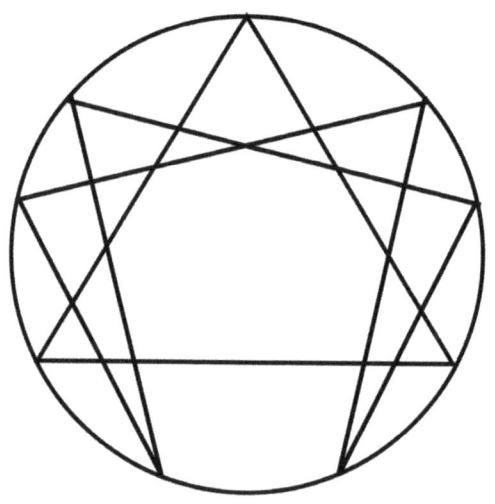

Part V

Strategies for Spending

Emotional Awareness of Spending

As we've established, money is emotional. Consider the following journal prompts on spending:

1. Recall your last purchase. What emotions show up when you think about it now?
2. When thinking of 1-2 purchases within the last month, what emotions do you recall feeling prior to shopping?
3. What emotions came up while spending?
4. What emotions showed up after spending?
5. What kind of spending brings up anxiety or guilt for you?
6. What are some things that bring you comfort or joy when spending money on them?

_____

_____

_____

_____

_____

_____

_____

_____

_____

_____

Enneagram Edge:
Self-Preservation Enneagram Subtype: How much of your spending plan is focused on comforts? What else do you need to prioritize?

Social Enneagram Subtype: Your spending plan is only a small part of a larger system of your finances. Does it provide more freedom to view it this way? What changes might you make when you view spending in this way?

One-to-One Enneagram Subtype: How does it feel to have a plan for the little things that bring you excitement in life? Practice being present to enhance enjoyment of the things you spend money on.

 *Financial Therapy Focus: Scale your emotions on a scale of 1-10 before, during, and after spending money. What's another option that changes your numbers for the better when sad, lonely, anxious, or tired?*

Spending Plan for Shutting Down Shame

MONTHLY INCOME	ESTIMATE/GOAL	ACTUAL EARNED
Salary/Wages Job 1		
Salary/Wages Job 2		
Bonus / Side Hustle		
Other Income		
TOTAL MONTHLY INCOME		

MONTHLY EXPENSES (FIXED)	ESTIMATE/GOAL	ACTUAL SPENT
Mortgage/Rent		
Car Loan Payments		
Car Insurance		
Credit Card Payment		
Student Loan Payment		
Life Insurance		
Cusion/Emergency		
Short Term Savings		
Childcare (if applicable)		
MONTHLY EXPENSES (FLEXIBLE)	ESTIMATE/GOAL	ACTUAL SPENT
Healthcare Costs (Copays/RX)		
Groceries		
Gas		
Phone		
Utilities		
Household Items		
Small Spend Joys		
Clothing		
Eating		
Entertainment		
Gifts/Birthdays		
Other		
TOTAL MONTHLY EXPENSES		

 *Financial Therapy Focus: Don't forget to identify your short-term savings goals and small spend joys to avoid deprivation!*

Values-Based Spending

Seeking clarity on what we want to spend our money on is enlightening to spending habits, whether it's small-spend joys or bigger savings goals. People prioritize spending money on things that are important to them, therefore completing a values exercise can add another layer of awareness to spending.

1. What values do you find most important in others?
2. Who is someone you respect or admire? Why?
3. Think of someone you don't like. What values do you think they hold?
4. What strengths do people say you possess? How do they describe you?
5. What feels most important in your personal life?
6. What feels most important in your professional life?
7. What values are you most proud to embody? Why?
8. If money wasn't a worry, what would you want to do for four hours a day?

_____

_____

_____

_____

_____

_____

_____

_____

_____

_____

_____

_____

Take a look at the list of values below, noticing any emotional response or pull towards particular words. What do they have in common with your responses to the list of questions above?

Personal Growth	Friendship	Purpose
Advancement and Promotion	Simplicity	Rationality
Challenge	Service	Power and Authority
Affection	Helping Others	Privacy
Authority	Neatness	Spiritual Growth
Competence	Honesty	Recognition
Perseverance	Independence	Adventure
Intelligence	Achievement	Self-acceptance
Having a Family	Helping Society	Competition
Creativity	Pleasure	Security
Inner Harmony	Self Control	Health
Public Service	Tradition	Wealth
Community	Appearance	Stability
Intimacy	Being Present	Belonging
Prosperity	Play	Diplomacy
Consensus	Communication	Respect
Teamwork	Wisdom	Environment
Fairness	Courage	Forgiveness
Peace	Integrity	Fame
Time Freedom	Tolerance	Education
Self-Respect	Religion	Order
Nature	Knowledge	Location
Leadership	Loyalty	Excellence
Ethical Practice	Taking Risks	Decisiveness
Cooperation	Excitement	Involvement
Being in a Family	Meaningful Work	Safety
Commitment	Happiness	Acceptance

My top 3 values _____   _____   _____

Does one value need your attention because it's currently absent in your life? Is there something that can shift to help you live more fully in your values?

Enneagram Edge:
Self-Preservation Enneagram Subtype: What values are you neglecting by your tendency to operate out of a need for safety and comfort?

Social Enneagram Subtype: Which values represent you as a person versus you as part of a family, friend or work group?

One-to-One Enneagram Subtype: What values make you feel most connected to those you care most about?

Financial Therapy Focus: Do your values anchor your spending choices for the here-and-now needs versus future plans? How can spending be adjusted to honor your values and what's most important to you?

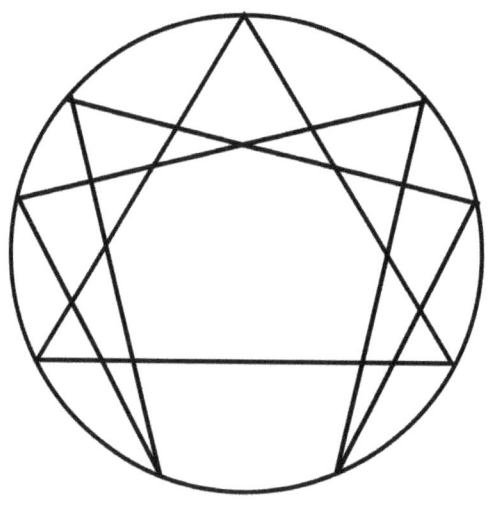

Part VI

Earn More Money

Money Mindset Shifts: My Future Relationship With Money

I. Revisit some of your money beliefs from the first exercise in this workbook. What would you prefer to believe about money?

_____

_____

_____

_____

II. My Future Relationship with Money

JOURNAL PROMPT

*   What do you want your future relationship with money to look like? How will it impact your relationships, your job, yourself?

*   Consider the Miracle Question: You wake up tomorrow and a miracle has happened! Your stressors around money are gone. What will be different?

_____

_____

_____

_____

_____

_____

_____

_____

_____

_____

Enneagram Edge:

Self-Preservation Enneagram Subtype: How would earning more money impact your anxiety? How can you shift your money mindset with your current net worth? Name what you already have, how does it feel?

Social Enneagram Subtype: Who can you connect with to find more opportunities for earning more money? Set yourself a goal to reach out to at least 1-2 of your named people this month.

One-to-One Enneagram Subtype: How can you channel your competitive side into creating new income streams? Can you connect with another person to engage in a true competition for making more money or is this an opportunity to be self-competitive?

 *Financial Therapy Focus: How close are you to your future relationship with money? What is one tool from this workbook that will get you one step closer to that future relationship with money?*

Naming Net Worth

What shows up for you when I ask you what your net worth is? It feels like a very personal question. This exercise is all about exploring the emotional elements AND knowing your numbers.

What do you have?

- Assets are things you own, including physical items of worth like jewelry and cars or houses you own as well as investments, stocks, and bonds.

- Liabilities are things you owe, like student loans, a car payment, credit card debt, a mortgage, etc.

Step 1: Loving the Lists

It's time to put your items in each column and their amounts. You can start with an estimation if you aren't sure of exact numbers just yet.

ASSETS	LIABILITIES

Step 2: Monitor the Math

Add up the numbers in your assets column (what you own) and add up your numbers in your liabilities column (what you owe).

Step 3: Discovering Your Debt

Subtract your liabilities from your assets. (Assets – Liabilities). You may have a negative number to start, indicating you have more liabilities that assets, meaning debt. This is normal and can be a starting place to monitor how your numbers change as you embrace financial strategies to reduce debt and increase your assets such as savings and investments.

Step 4: Review and Revise

Review this exercise quarterly to see how the numbers change. Are you seeing the amount of debt decline? Seeing the numbers shift is something to celebrate!

Enneagram Edge:
Self-Preservation Enneagram Subtype: What emotions are associated with this exercise? Notice where you store those emotions in your body. Practice breath-work while processing these feelings and remember to ground yourself. You might repeat the mantra, "Even though things feel scary, I am safe."

Social Enneagram Subtype: When you consider your whole financial system, how does that help you better conceptualize your goals? What is the most important part of the system to focus on at this time? What emotions come up as you think about these things?

One-to-One Enneagram Subtype: You may want to make a quick decision about what to go and do now. Slow down and process before you choose to change anything. Sit on your numbers for a few days and let everything sink in before you move into action. What is it like for you to practice slowing down and waiting? Lean into those feelings.

Financial Therapy Focus: Although financial professionals would say this is a concrete exercise of numbers, financial therapists would consider it a marker for progress as you see the numbers change, revisiting your numbers as often as is helpful to your financial goals.

Loud Budgeting

Have you heard of loud budgeting? It's about saying no and maintaining money boundaries for yourself and with others. It can sound like:

I don't want to prioritize that right now.
I don't want to spend money on that.
That's not a priority.
I have other goals in mind right now.
I'm saving my money for xxx.
I've already met my budget this month for (coffee/eating out/shopping/etc).
No thank you.

What are some social scenarios where you might need to say no to spending money? Write them down as well as your responses for practice and increased confidence!

_____

_____

_____

_____

_____

_____

_____

Enneagram Edge:

Self-Preservation Enneagram Subtype: Where might you exercise your ability to say "yes" more? Choose one area to "splurge" on yourself that you usually don't allow yourself to. What physical comfort might you say "no" to this month?

Social Enneagram Subtype: How might you say "yes" to something that helps you feel more connected to your community? Where might you need to say "no" to your community? How do each of these scenarios make you feel? What might that tell you about a potential growth opportunity for yourself?

One-to-One Enneagram Subtype: You have a propensity towards intensity. How might you hold each category with more curiosity when choosing your "yeses" and "nos" rather than making quick decisions?

 *Financial Therapy Focus: Exploring your yes and no to spending money can be strengthened by revisiting your values. Is this spending aligned with your values? It may feel like an enthusiastic yes! Is this spending not in alignment with your values? Practice saying no.*

Making Money Buckets

Many of the money apps and tools out there talk about a percentage of expenses going into various categories or buckets, such as basic needs, wants, needs, savings, and future planning, just to name a few. Let's name your buckets based on what speaks to you!

Step 1: Name Your Buckets

For your everyday expenses and predictable monthly debts, the bucket will be called (everyday living, basic needs, etc.)

_____

For your self-care bucket, for things that enhance your lifestyle and nourish you mind, body and spirit, the bucket will be called (self-care, restoration, nourish, etc.)

_____

For your future bucket, capturing things that relate to retirement, money goals like owning a house, six weeks off, or starting a family, the bucket will be called (freedom, my future, retirement, etc.)

_____

Step 2: Record Expenses

Now that you've named your buckets, it's time to put your expenses (and the costs) in them.

Examples of everyday expenses and predictable monthly debts include food, a rent or mortgage, car payment, minimum credit card payments, insurances, etc.

Examples of self-care items may include gym membership, massage, going out to eat, ski pass, manicure, shopping, sports equipment, club dues, food subscriptions, etc.

Examples of future items might be a retirement plan, SEP, 401K, investment portfolio, stocks, bonds, savings, and inheritance.

Step 3: Know Your Numbers

Calculate your monthly income. For example, let's say you make $4000 per month and have $2800 in expenses in your basic needs bucket, $1000 in your self-care bucket, and $0 in your future planning bucket.

The goal for your buckets is a 50-30-20 split. Financial professionals would normalize 50% of your income is expected to cover your basic needs.

In our example, 50% of $4,000 income is $2,000. A 30% self-care bucket would mean $1,200 and 20% future planning is $800.

What are your current percentages? Does this exercise provide a snapshot of where your buckets are now and if there are any changes you want to make over time?

_____
(name)

_____
(percentage)

_____
(name)

_____
(percentage)

_____
(name)

_____
(percentage)

Enneagram Edge:

Self-Preservation Enneagram Subtype: What might you be able to sacrifice from your "self-care" bucket? Is there something that you can put into your "future" bucket instead? What does it feel like to choose to focus on something that is not concrete?

Social Enneagram Subtype: How might you choose to include your community in these exercises? Does framing the goals for each bucket to include your family/community change the way you want to allocate your expenses?

One-to-One Enneagram Subtype: What's it like for you to slow down and be very concrete about your expenses? What do you notice about how you are currently spending your money? What might you want to change?

Financial Therapy Focus: The percentages are not important. We repeat, not important! This exercise is more about each expense having a home in one of the buckets, and having balance in having all buckets represented in your life currently to avoid deprivation.

Tasks or Time-Freedom

What does it cost for one hour of our time compared to paying someone else? Is it worth the investment of paying another person for delegated tasks? Does it improve our mental health? As someone who is starting to make more money, the questions you may ask yourself to embrace more time freedom might sound like this:

1. What is the task that needs to get done?
2. How much time does the task require?
3. How enjoyable or unenjoyable is this task for me on a scale of 1 to 10 (1 very unenjoyable, 10 the most enjoyable)
4. What does it cost for me to do it? What would it cost for someone else to do it?
5. Do I want someone else to do it?

_____

_____

_____

_____

_____

_____

_____

Enneagram Edge:

Self-Preservation Enneagram Subtype: You often want to live simply and be frugal with your money. What does it bring up for you to consider paying someone else to do something that you are capable of doing but might be able to delegate? When you consider what would be most helpful to hire out for, what comes to mind? What would it feel like to call someone today?

Social Enneagram Subtype: What would it be like to work with someone to accomplish some of the responsibilities you hold? What does it feel like to ask for help? What might you learn from acting on this?

One-to-One Enneagram Subtype: When asking someone else to assist you, things might not get done the way that you would do them. What's it like to think about letting go of the expectations you have for yourself/others and practice gratitude for the time that it gives back to you?

 *Financial Therapy Focus: Time and money are both valuable. Don't forget the value of asking, "at what cost?" when making time vs. price decisions.*

Congratulations! You've just worked your way through 23 exercises to have a better relationship with your money! Check out your Enneagram edges alongside these exercises in our book Your Enneagram and Money: Transforming Enneagram Edges into Financial Freedom and share with us what you've discovered at our Facebook group Your Enneagram and Money.

About the Authors

Khara is an 8x published author who is passionate about turning pain points into possibilities. This means she loves talking about topics others wish to avoid, like leadership trauma, client suicide, and money challenges. As a Social Enneagram Type Three wing Two, perfectionist, financial therapist and serial entrepreneur who specializes in working with helping professionals, of course she wanted to write a book and a workbook to help colleagues unlock their money flow and full potential instead of facing chronic burnout. The Enneagram has been a part of Khara's therapy practice for more than 13 years and is now part of her financial therapy practice for therapists. She hopes the skills and tools we explore together in this workbook will help you to break free of money shame and scarcity to allow financial health and wellness into your life instead.

Hannah, a Self-Preservation Three, is a Licensed Professional Counselor, Certified Enneagram Coach and career counselor. She loves helping people find passion, motivation, and fulfillment in their personal and professional lives, which is why the Enneagram fits so naturally into her therapy practice. She has been using the Enneagram for over a decade and has seen her clients' lives transform through their experience of this tool. Hannah loves helping people get out of their own way so that they can succeed, and her support of this workbook does just that.

JOURNEY INSTITUTE PRESS

Journey Institute Press is a non-profit publishing house created by authors to flip the publishing model for new authors. Created with intention and purpose to provide the highest quality publishing resources available to authors whose stories might otherwise not be told.
JI Press focusses on women, BIPOC, and LGBTQ+ authors without regard to the genre of their work.
As a Publishing House, our goal is to create a supportive, nurturing, and encouraging environment that puts the author above the publisher in the publishing model.
Guide Point North Publishing is an Imprint of Journey Institute Press, a division of 50 in 52 Journey, Inc.

THE
JOURNEY
INSTITUTE
PRESS